O Holy Night

Thirty Christmas Songs for High Voice & Organ

Edited by Neil Jenkins

Kevin Mayhew

We hope you enjoy *O Holy Night* (High Voice Edition).
Further copies of this are available from your local
music shop or Christian bookshop.

In case of difficulty, please contact the publisher direct:

The Sales Department
KEVIN MAYHEW LTD
Rattlesden
Bury St Edmunds
Suffolk IP30 0SZ

Phone 01449 737978
Fax 01449 737834

Please ask for our complete catalogue of outstanding Church Music.

Acknowledgements

The publishers wish to express their gratitude to the following
for permission to reproduce copyright material in this book:

Boosey & Hawkes Music Publishers Ltd, The Hyde, Edgware Road, London NW9 6JN for *The Little Road to Bethlehem* © 1946 Boosey & Co Ltd, *I sing of a maiden* © 1924 Winthrop Rogers Ltd, *Whence is that goodly fragrance* (music) © 1922 Boosey & Co Ltd, *Balulalow* (Howells) © 1923 Winthrop Rogers Ltd, *The Oxen* © 1952 Boosey & Co Ltd and *Lowly, laid in a manger* © 1938 Hawkes & Son (London) Ltd.

Cramer Music Ltd, 23 Garrick Street, London WC2E 9AX for *When the herds were watching* © 1948 Cramer Music Ltd.

Magdalene College, Cambridge CB3 0AG for *Whence is that goodly fragrance* (text).

For the USA only: Oxford University Press, Walton Street, Oxford OX2 6DP for *Adam lay ybounden* © 1922 Oxford University Press, *Balulalow* (Warlock) © 1919 Oxford University Press, *Where riches is everlastingly* © 1928 Oxford University Press.

First published in Great Britain in 1994 by Kevin Mayhew Ltd

ISBN 0 86209 556 5
Catalogue No: 1450021

Front Cover: *The Holy Family* by Pieter van Avont (1600-1632).
Reproduced by courtesy of Fine Art Photographic Library, London.
Cover designed by Juliette Clarke and Graham Johnstone
Picture Research: Jane Rayson

Music Editor: Anthea Smith
Music Setting: Chris Hinkins

Printed and bound in Great Britain

Contents

Foreword

I hope that *O Holy Night* will be a welcome addition to the ever-growing list of collections of seasonal music. We have gathered together under one cover thirty of the best Christmas solo songs, newly arranged with organ accompaniments. This will be of interest to anyone planning the music for a Christmas concert, carol service, or Christmas worship.

O Holy Night by Adolphe Adam heads a list of French classics that also includes Gounod's *Nazareth* and Benjamin Godard's famous *Berceuse,* newly set to the favourite carol text *Sing Lullaby.*

There is a strong representation of German song too, since this volume contains all of Peter Cornelius's *Christmas Songs* Op. 8 in new English versions. The most famous of these is his *The Three Kings,* which is so well known in its choral adaptation. Here we include it in its original version for solo voice, where, according to Cornelius himself, the inspiration for its chorale accompaniment came from Franz Liszt. Another song with a chorale accompaniment is Max Reger's *Glory to God,* which is included alongside his better-known *The Virgin's Slumber Song.*

In this volume too can be found all the favourites from the English twentieth century school – settings by Ireland, Warlock, Armstrong Gibbs, Quilter, Howells and Michael Head. There are rarities as well; little-known songs by Stanford, Frederick Keel and William Hurlstone (who died at the early age of thirty after having displayed enormous promise as a composer).

Many of these songs can be effectively sung by unison voices – *Mater Ora Filium* and *Personent Hodie* frequently are. In addition, I have provided optional SA choral parts for some of the pieces. *O Holy Night* has an optional two-part refrain, and *Where riches is everlastingly* a three-part chorus. I have added a unison chorale melody part in *Glory to God,* to represent the choir of distant angels, whilst Malcolm Archer has added an optional descant to his arrangement of *Child in the Manger.*

I am grateful to Charles Macdonald for his assistance in preparing this volume.

NEIL JENKINS

CHILD IN THE MANGER

Text: Mary MacDonald (1817-1890) trans. Lachlan Macbean (1853-1931)
Music: Traditional Gaelic melody arranged Malcolm Archer (b.1952)

* The right hand of the organ part, when not accompanying the voices, may be played on a flute or oboe.

fall.
Gt.
mp
tr
Once the most ho - ly child of sal - va - tion, gen - tle and low - ly, lived be-
Sw.
low; now as our glo - rious migh-ty re - dee - mer, see him vic - to - rious o'er each
foe.
Gt. mf

Descant (optional)
Melody
Ah,
Pro-phets fore-told him, in-fant of
Gt.
Ped.
Ah,
won - der; an-gels be-hold him on his throne;
Ah,
wor-thy our
cresc.
rall.
Ah.
Sa - viour of all their prai - ses; hap-py for e - ver are his own.
ff

SING LULLABY

Text: Sabine Baring-Gould (1834-1924) adapted Neil Jenkins
Music: Benjamin Godard (1849-1895) arr. Neil Jenkins

pp
pier - cing. Lul - la - by, lul - la - by; then in the grave re - pos - ing.
pp
Andante
p
1,2 Hush! Do not wake the in - fant king.
Soon will come sor - row with the mor - ning.
Soon will come bit - ter grief and weep - ing. Sing

rall.
lul - la - by, ba - by now a-sleep -
rall.
a tempo
ing. Hush! Hush!
a tempo
for soon will come the mor - ning.
1. to verse 2
2. Fine
Lul - la - by! Sing lul - la - by! lul - la - by!

Andantino
rall.
quasi recit.
p
2. Hush,
Verse 2
rall.
a tempo
mp
do not stir the in-fant king. Sing lul - la - by! Sing lul - la, lul-la - by! The
a tempo
p
ba - by's now a doz - ing, dream-ing of Ea - ster mor-ning, glad-some Ea-ster
Ped. ad lib.
pp
D.S. al Fine
mor - ning; con-qu'ring death, con-qu'ring death, and all its bon-dage break - ing.
pp

LOWLY, LAID IN A MANGER

Text: Herbert S Brown
Music: John Ireland (1879-1962)

dor - ing, the boy, the heav'n - ly child, the heav'n - ly child.
p
pp
p
Leave your work and your play - time and kneel in ho - mage and prayer, the Prince of Love is
p
Man.
Ped.
smil - ing a - sleep in his cra - dle there. Bend your heart to the won - der, the
Man.
mf
birth, the my - ste - ry mild, and wor - ship, si - lent, a - dor - ing, the boy, the heav'n - ly
mf
Ped.

pp
child, the heav'n-ly child. Dim the light of the lan - tern, and bare the mean a-
p
pp
Man.
Ped.
p
bode, yet gold and myrrh and in - cense pro - claim the son of God.
p
f
Low - ly laid in a man - ger by Vir - gin un - de - filed, come wor - ship, si - lent, a -
f
Man.
Ped.
p
rall.
dor - ing, the boy, the heav'n-ly child, the heav'n-ly child.
rall.
p
pp
Man.
Ped.

THE SHEPHERDS (Version 1)

Text: Peter Cornelius (1824-1874) trans. Neil Jenkins
Music: Peter Cornelius (1824-1874) arr. Neil Jenkins

p
On - ly the shep - herds, the hum - ble shep - herds, their lone - ly
On - ly the shep - herds, the hum - ble shep - herds, learned of this
poco rall.
watch were keep - ing.
great sal - va - tion.
poco rall.
con moto
p
Man.
mf
p
2. And lo! there came a host on high of an - gels sing - ing in the
4. And prais - ing God the shep - herds went to see the gift which God had
p
Ped.

f
sky: 'Good-will to men u - pon the Earth. Be not a -
sent with - in that sta - ble low - ly. Wor - ship him,
f
Man.
dim.
fraid, for I bring you glad ti - dings, glad ti - dings of your Mes - si -
shep - herds, you hum - ble shep - herds, O wor - ship your Sa - viour ho -
dim.
Ped.
poco rall.
con moto
- ah's birth.'
- ly.
con moto
poco rall.
pp
legato
p
Man.
pp

THE SHEPHERDS (Version 2)

Text: Peter Cornelius (1824-1874) trans. Neil Jenkins
Music: Peter Cornelius (1824-1874) arr. Neil Jenkins

wak - ing till day-light is break - ing.
mf
p
Lo! the an-gels ap-pear,
cresc. poco a poco
bid-ding them ba-nish all fear,
Ped.
with the sto-ry of Christ Je-sus' glo - ry, the
mf
f
sto - ry of Christ Je-sus' glo - ry.
poco rit.

a tempo
mf
Se - raphs sing in the sky: 'Praise
the Fa - ther on high! For each na - tion shall now find sal -
Solo
va - tion,
p
each na - tion shall
now find sal - va - tion!'
Più mosso
Quick-ly the

shep - herds run to see God's on - ly son
Tempo I
mf
ly - ing ho - ly in man - ger so low - ly,
p
ly - ing ho - ly in man - ger so
f
low - ly.
mf
p

PERSONENT HODIE

Latin Text: *Piae Cantiones* (1582)
English Text: Jane Joseph (1894-1929)
Music: Gustav Holst (1874-1934)

Alternative Text:

1. On this day earth shall ring
   with the song children sing
   to the son, Christ the King,
   born on earth to save us;
   him the Father gave us.
   Ideo gloria in excelsis Deo!

2. His the doom, ours the mirth,
   when he came down to earth;
   Bethlehem saw his birth;
   ox and ass, beside him,
   from the cold would hide him.
   Ideo gloria in excelsis Deo!

3. God's bright star, o'er his head,
   wise men three to him led;
   kneel they low by his bed,
   lay their gifts before him,
   praise him and adore him.
   Ideo gloria in excelsis Deo!

4. On this day angels sing;
   with their song earth shall ring,
   praising Christ, heaven's King,
   born on earth to save us;
   peace and love he gave us.
   Ideo gloria in excelsis Deo!

THE STAR OF BETHLEHEM

Text: Frederick Edward Weatherly (1848-1929)
Music: Stephen Adams (1844-1913) arr. Neil Jenkins

saw the bright stars shine, and child - hood came a - gain to me, with
rall.
all its dreams di - vine.
a tempo
Then, as I list - ened to the bells, and
p
Ped.
watched the skies a - far, out of the East ma - je - sti - cal there
rose one ra - diant star; and ev - 'ry o - ther star grew pale be -
poco accel.

cantabile
fore that heav'n-ly glow, it seemed to bid me fol - low, and I
cantabile
f
could not choose but go, it seemed to bid me
f
p tranquillo
fol - low, and I could not choose but go.
p
f

p quasi parlando
From street to street it led me, by ma-ny a man-sion fair, it
Man.
shone through din-gy case-ment on ma-ny a gar-ret bare; from high-way on to high-way, through
rall.
al-leys dark and cold, and where it shone the dark-ness was flood-ed all with gold.
rall.
a tempo
dolce
Sad hearts for-got their sor - row, rough hearts grew soft and mild, and
a tempo
p
Ped.

wea - ry lit - tle chil - dren turned in their sleep and smiled; while
poco accel.
ma - ny a home - less wan - der - er up - lift - ed pa - tient eyes
poco accel.
cantabile
seem - ing to see a home at last be - yond those star - ry
cantabile
f
skies,
f
seem - ing to see a home at last be -
f
p
p

tranquillo
yond those star - ry skies.
f
p
And
Più mosso
then me-thought earth fa - ded, I rose as borne on wings, be -
p
Man.
poco animato
yond the waste of ru - ined lives, the press of hu - man things; a -

cresc.
bove the toil and sha - dow, a - bove the want and woe, my
molto rall.
old self and its dark - ness seemed left on earth be -
molto rall.
cresc.
Ped.
a tempo
p
low. And on - ward, up - ward shone the star, un -
a tempo
p
cresc.
til it seemed to me, it flashed u - pon the
cresc.

molto rall.
ff
gol - den gate, and o'er the cry - stal sea; and
molto rall.
Tempo I
con forza
then the gates rolled back - ward, I stood where an - gels trod; it was the
colla voce
f
dim.
grandioso
cresc.
star, the star of Beth - le - hem had led me up to God, the star, the
f
mf
p
cresc.
rit.
f
star had led me up to God.
rit.
f

BALULALOW

Text: Martin Luther (1483-1546) trans. the brothers Wedderburn (1567)
Music: Peter Warlock (1894-1930) arr. Charles Macdonald

poco rit.
a tempo
mp
But I sall praise thee
poco rit.
a tempo
mp
e - ver - more with sang - is sweet un - to thy gloir; the
knees of my heart sall I bow, and sing that richt Ba -
poco rit.
lu - la - low!
poco rit.
pp
molto rit.
ppp

THE LITTLE ROAD TO BETHLEHEM

Text: Margaret Rose

Music: Michael Head (1900-1976) arr. Charles Macdonald

side an o - pen door, as I drew nigh, I heard sweet Ma - ry sing a lul - la -
p
by. She sang a - bout the lambs at close of day and rocked her ti - ny king a - mong the
3
hay. A - cross the air the sil - ver sheep - bell rang: 'The
pp
Solo (4′ Fl.)
pp
Man.
Ped.
Poco meno mosso
lambs are com - ing home,' sweet Ma - ry sang. 'Your star of gold, your star of gold is

Tempo I
shin- ing in the sky, so sleep, my lit - tle king, go lul - la - by.'
Solo
Man.
pp
As I walked down the road at set of sun, the
pp
Ped.
lambs were com - ing home - wards, one by one. I heard a sheep - bell soft - ly cal - ling
rit. e dim.
them a - long the lit - tle road to Beth - le - hem.
rit.
dim.
pp
Man.
Ped.

THE THREE KINGS (Version 1)

Text: Peter Cornelius (1824-1874) trans. Herbert Newell Bate (1871-1941)
Music: Peter Cornelius (1824-1874) arr. Neil Jenkins

king; gold, in - cense, myrrh are their of - fer - ing. The star shines
out with a stead - fast ray: the kings to Beth - le - hem make their way, and there in
wor - ship they bend the knee, as Ma - ry's child in her lap they see;
their ro - yal gifts they show to the king; gold, in - cense, myrrh are their

of - fer - ing. Thou child of man! Lo, to Beth - le - hem
Un poco più mosso
the kings are trav'l - ling, tra - vel with them! The star of mer - cy, the star of
p
grace shall lead thy heart to its rest - ing place. Gold, in - cense, myrrh thou canst not
rit.
rit.
a tempo
bring; of - fer thy heart to the in - fant king. Of - fer thy heart!
a tempo
f
p

THE THREE KINGS (Version 2)

Text: Peter Cornelius (1824-1874) trans. Herbert Newell Bate (1871-1941)
Music: Peter Cornelius (1824-1874) arr. Neil Jenkins

tra - vel- lers three, where the new - born king of the Jews may be. Full
bend the knee, as Ma - ry's child in her lap they see; their
star of grace shall lead thy heart to its rest - ing place. Gold,
ro - yal gifts they bear for the king; gold, in - cense, myrrh are their of - fer - ing.
ro - yal gifts they show to the king; gold, in - cense, myrrh are their of - fer - ing.
in - cense, myrrh thou canst not bring; of - fer thy heart to the in - fant king.
più f
p
Ped.
p

MATER ORA FILIUM

Text: 15th century
Music: Charles Wood (1866-1926)

mp dolce
1. Fair mai - den, who is this bairn that thou bear - est in thine arm?
2. Man to fa - ther he hath none, but him - self God a - lone;
mp
Sir, it is a king - is son, that in heav'n a - bove doth won.*
of a mai - den he would be born, to save man - kind that was for - lorn.
p
Ma - ter o - ra fi - li - um, ut post hoc ex - i - li - um, no - bis do - net
p
gau - di - um be - a - to - rum om - ni - um.

* won = dwell

3. Three kings brought him pre - sents; gold, myrrh, and frank - in - cense
to my son full of might, King of kings and Lord of right.
Ma - ter o - ra fi - li - um, ut post hoc ex - i - li - um, no - bis do - net
gau - di - um be - a - to - rum om - ni - um.
Ped.
Man.

p
4. Fair maiden pray for us unto thy son, sweet Jesus, that
Ped.
rall.
he will send us of his grace in heav'n on high to have a place.
a tempo
pp
Mater ora filium, ut post hoc exilium, nobis donet
Man.
mp
gaudium beatorum omnium.
rall. e dim.
dim.
ppp
Ped.

BETHLEHEM DOWN

Text: Bruce Blunt (1899-1957)
Music: Peter Warlock (1894-1930) arr. Charles Macdonald

fair with her first - born on Beth - le - hem Down.
pp
Beth - le - hem Down is full of the star - light,
pp
Man.
p
winds for the spi - ces, and stars for the gold,
p
Ped.
ppp
Ma - ry for sleep, and for lul - la - by mu - sic:
ppp legatissimo

pp
songs of a shep - herd by Beth - le - hem fold.
pp
3 4
ppp
6 4
When he is king, they will clothe him in grave-sheets,
8
ppp
Man.
myrrh for em - bal - ming, and wood for a crown,
pp
he that lies now in the
8
pp
Ped.
ppp
white arms of Ma - ry, sleep - ing so light - ly on

rit.
Beth - le - hem Down.
cresc.
a tempo
p
Here he has peace and a short while for dream-ing, close-hud-dled ox - en to
keep him from cold, Ma - ry for love, and for lul - la-by mu - sic:
mf
pp
ppp
rall.
songs of a shep-herd by Beth - le - hem fold.
dim.

THE VIRGIN'S SLUMBER SONG

Text: Martin Boelitz trans. Neil Jenkins
Music: Max Reger (1873-1916)

rit.
a tempo
Je - sus, sweet - ly sleep.
dolcissimo
p
Ra-diant is the lit-tle smile on your lips as now you rest.
pp
Lay your gol-den head a-while on your gen-tle mo-ther's breast.
mf
Sleep, lit - tle Je - sus, sweet - ly sleep.

CHRIST, THE FRIEND OF CHILDREN

Text: Peter Cornelius (1824-1874) trans. Neil Jenkins
Music: Peter Cornelius (1824-1874) arr. Neil Jenkins

hear we; their mean-ing try to un - der stand.
'Suf - fer the chil - dren to come near me: they shall in - he - rit God's own
mf
land.'
mp
This is the sea-son of the
Solo
Ped.
p
Man.
year to pon - der on those say-ings dear,
when me - mo - ries of child-hood
Ped.
Man.

days are co - vered with a dis - tant haze. Now all the Christ - mas lights are
mf
Ped.
Man.
glow - ing I seem to be a child a - gain.
Oh, would that I were with them go - ing to see the place where Christ shall
mf
reign!
Solo
Ped.

BALULALOW

Text: Martin Luther (1483-1586) trans. the brothers Wedderburn (1567)
Music: Herbert Howells (1892-1983) arr. Charles Macdonald

part.
But
I sall praise thee e - ver -
more with sang - is sweet un - to thy
gloir; the knees of my heart
mp
pp
Ped.
mf
mp
Man.

pp
sall I bow, and sing,
p
and sing that richt Ba -
Ped.
sempre dim.
pp
lu - la - low! Ba - lu - la -
poco rall.
low!
poco rall.
ppp
ppp

NAZARETH

Text: Henry F Chorley
Music: Charles Gounod (1818-1893) arr. Neil Jenkins

more, life for e - ver - more, life for e - ver -
p
more.
mf
Shep - herds who fol - ded your flocks be -
p
Man.
side you, tell what was told by an - gel voi - ces

near: 'To you this night is born he who will
guide you through paths of peace to liv - ing wa - ters
clear.' Though poor be the cham - ber, come here, come and a -
dore; Lo! the Lord of Hea - ven

hath to mor - tals gi - ven life for e - ver -
Ped.
more.
p
mf
Kings from a far land, draw near and be -
p
Man.
hold him, led by the beam whose warn - ing bade ye
tr
Ped.

come; your crowns cast down, with
robe ro - yal en - fold him, your king de -
pp
Man.
Ped.
scends to earth from bright - er home.
rit.
a tempo
Though poor be the cham - ber, come here, come and a - dore;
pp

Lo! the Lord of Hea - ven hath to mor - tals
gi - ven life for e - ver - more.
p
Ped.
mp
Wind to the ce - dars pro -
Man.
claim the joy - ful sto - ry, wave of the

sea, the ti - dings bear a - far. The
night is gone! Be - hold in all its
cresc.
Ped.
glo - ry all broad and bright ri - ses th'e-
ter - nal morn - ing star. Though poor be the
cresc.
rit.
a tempo
ff

cham - ber, come here, come and a - dore;
Lo! the Lord of Hea - ven hath to mor - tals
gi - ven life for e - ver - more, life for e - ver -
p
more, life for e - ver - more!
rit.

THE CHRIST CHILD

Text: Peter Cornelius (1824-1874) trans. Neil Jenkins
Music: Peter Cornelius (1824-1874) arr. Neil Jenkins

When he came down from Hea - ven's height, this sin - ful world was filled with
light.
Then let us all with
one ac - cord give prai - ses to the in - fant Lord.
The
Solo
Ped.
Man.
Ped.
Man.

f
Christ - mas can - dles are a - glow, while loud 'No - els' from or - gans blow!
Solo f
f
p
Ped.
Man.
mf
mf
Lord Je - sus comes to great and small; he pours his bles - sings on us all.
p
mf
p

mf
Then give him thanks with heart and voice, for this is the day all Chris-tians re-
p
mf
joice,
Solo
Ped.
Man.
for
f
this is the day Chris - tians re - joice!
dim.
f
mf
Ped.
mp
poco rit.
a tempo
p
f

ADAM LAY YBOUNDEN

Text: from the Sloane manuscript (c.15th century)
Music: Peter Warlock (1894-1930) arr. Charles Macdonald

Rather slower
fin - den writ - ten in their book. Ne had one ap - ple ta - ken been, the
Tempo I
ap - ple ta - ken been, ne had ne - ver Our La - dy a been hea - ven's
pochiss. rit.
a tempo
mf
queen. Bles - sèd be the time that ap - ple ta - ken was.
f
ff allargando
There - fore we moun sing - en: De - o gra - ti - as!
allargando
ff

WHENCE IS THAT GOODLY FRAGRANCE

Text: trans. from the French by Allen Beville Ramsey (1872-1955)
Music: Samuel Liddle (1868-1951) arr. Neil Jenkins

poco rit.
sen - ses all a - way?
poco rit.
dolce
Poco più mosso
What is that light so bril - liant, break - ing here in the night a - cross our eyes?
Man.
cresc.
Ne - ver so bright, the day - star wak - ing, star - ted to climb the mor - ning
poco cresc.
skies! What is that light so bril - liant, break - ing here in the night a -

molto rall.
a tempo
p
cross our eyes? Beth-le-hem! There in man-ger ly-ing,
molto rall.
a tempo
pp
Ped.
sim.
find your Re-deem-er, haste a-way; run ye with ea-ger foot-steps
Man.
hie-ing! Wor-ship the Sa-viour born to-day. Beth-le-hem! There in
pp dolce
Ped.
man-ger ly-ing, find your Re-deem-er, haste a-way.
rit.

GLORY TO GOD

Text: Ludwig Hamann trans. Neil Jenkins
Chorale Text: Catherine Winkworth (1827-1878)
Music: Max Reger (1873-1916) arr. Neil Jenkins

pp
Bright - ly dawns for man the mor - row that will ba - nish pain and sor - row;
pp
Man.
Ped.
p cresc.
that will raise his soul on high.
p cresc.
f
f
pp
Man.
rit.
a tempo
pp
p
Solo
Hear the an - gels in the sky: 'Glo - ry to God in the high - est,
Chorus (Optional)
Sopranos and Altos
rit.
p
a tempo
(Hum)
rit.
a tempo
p

peace be u - pon earth, peace be u - pon earth,
and to all man-kind good-will be gi - ven.' Comes the
new hea - ven u - pon the earth? Dawns the pro - mised age of
p
pp
Ped.
Man.

f
gold? Will this peace be e - ver - last - ing, as the
pp
f
p
Ped.
p
an - gel - host fore - told? Christ - mas hope and Christ - mas
pp
Man.
cresc.
f
bles - sing ev - 'ry heart should be ex - pres - sing! Rich or hum - ble, great or small! Joy - ful,
cresc.
f
Ped.

rit.
a tempo
Solo
joy - ful be ye Chris - tians all! Glo - ry to God in the high - est;
Chorus
(Hum)
Man.
peace be u - pon earth, peace be u - pon earth, and to all man-kind good-
will be gi - ven. Now the say - ing of I - sai - ah
Ped.
Man.

p
is ful-filled for all on earth: 'All shall live! Your great Mes-
Ped.
si-ah will re-deem you by his birth, will re-deem you by his
pp
birth. For his mer-cy lasts for-e-ver, and his good-ness fail-eth ne-ver.'
Man.
Ped.
f cresc.
ff
There-fore let us now re-joice,
cresc.
ff
pp
Man.

Solo
Chorus
rit.
a tempo
giv - ing praise with heart and voice! Glo - ry to God in the high - est;
From heav'n a - bove to earth I come, to
peace be u - pon earth, peace be u - pon earth,
bear good news to ev - 'ry home. Glad ti - dings of great joy I bring; where -
and to all man-kind good - will be gi - ven.
of I now will say and sing.
Ped.
p
f
ff

THE OXEN

Text: Thomas Hardy (1840-1928)
Music: Cecil Armstrong Gibbs (1889-1960) arr. Charles Macdonald

em - bers in hearth - side ease.
Ped.
mf
We pic - tured the meek mild crea - tures
mf
sim.
as they dwelt in their straw - y pen,
p
nor did it oc - cur to one of us there to doubt they were kneel - ing
p
Man.

mf
then.
So fair a
fan - cy few would weave in these years!
mf
p
Ped.
Yet I feel if some - one said on Christ - mas Eve,
Gt.
Man.
Poco più mosso
f
'Come, see the
sim.

ox - en kneel in the lone - ly bar - ton by
poco rit.
p
yon - der coomb our child - hood used to know,
poco rit.
Sw. p
Tempo I
pp
I should go with him in the gloom,
mf
p
hop - ing it might be so.
pp
mf
pp
pp
Man.
Ped.
ppp

WHERE RICHES IS EVERLASTINGLY

Text: Anon medieval poem
Music: Peter Warlock (1894-1930) arr. Neil Jenkins

* Either take the Solo line alone, or divide into a 3-part chorus.

3. A sta - ble was his cham - ber, a cratch was his bed, he
4. A no - ble les - son here is us taught, to
had not a pil - low to lay un - der his head; with mai - den's milk that
set all world - ly ri - ches at naught, but pray we that we may
Refrain
babe was fed, in poor clothes was lap - ped the Lord Al - migh - ty.
be thi - ther brought where ri - ches is e - ver - las - ting - ly.
I

mp
pray you be mer - ry and sing with me in wor - ship of Christ's na -
mp
ff
mp
(2nd time ff)
Solo
ti - vi - ty. I pray you be mer - ry and sing with me in
Sopranos and Altos
orus
I pray you be mer - ry and sing with me in
1.
2.
wor - ship of Christ's na - ti - vi - ty. ti - vi - ty.

CRADLE SONG

Text: Traditional Spanish
Music: William Yeates Hurlstone (1876-1906) arr. Charles Macdonald

lord St Jo - a-chim, they rock the ba - by's cra - dle, that sleep may
come to him. Then sleep thou too, my ba - by, my
lit - tle heart so dear; the Vir - gin is be - side thee, the Son of
God is near.
Man.
Ped.
rit.
a tempo
rall.

I SING OF A MAIDEN

Text: 15th century

Music: Roger Quilter (1877-1953) arr. Charles Macdonald

* original: makeless

† original: ches

still there his mo - ther was, as dew in A - pril that fall - eth on the
grass. He came all so still to his mo - ther's bow'r, as
dew in A - pril that fall-eth on the flow'r. He came all so still
dolce
pp
Man.
Ped.

dolcissimo
rit.
there his mo-ther lay, as dew in A - pril that fall-eth on the spray.
rit.
a tempo
mp sonoro
Mo - ther and mai - den was ne - ver none but she; well may such a la - dy
a tempo
mp
p
p
Man.
God - dés mo - ther be.
p
pp
Ped.

THE CHRISTMAS TREE

Text: Peter Cornelius (1824-1874)
trans. Herbert Newell Bate (1871-1941) and Neil Jenkins
Music: Peter Cornelius (1824-1874) arr. Neil Jenkins

mo - ther sings of the Lord's good grace, where - by the child who re - deemed our race was
mf
born and a - dored in a low - ly place. Once
p
more the shep - herds, as she sings, bend low, and an - gels touch their strings: with
p
Man.
'Glo - ry' they hail the King of kings. The chil - dren list-en-ing
pp
Ped.
Man.

cresc.
round the tree can hear the heav'n - ly min - strel - sy, the man - ger's
cresc.
Ped.
mf
mar - vel they all can see. At this joy - ful time the hou - ses are bright to
mf
f
wel - come Je - sus, the God of Light! A sea - son of cheer: the ho - li - est
night.
mp
cresc.
f

WHEN THE HERDS WERE WATCHING

Text: William Canton (1845-1926)
Music: Frederick Keel (1871-1954) arr. Neil Jenkins

rall.
a tempo
dropped a rose of gold.
rall.
a tempo
mf
Ped.
p
When 'twas bit - ter win - ter, house - less and for - lorn, in a star - lit sta - ble
p
cresc.
f
Christ the babe was born. Wel - come, heav'n - ly lamb - kin, wel - come, gol - den rose;
cresc.
f
Man.
con entusiasmo
rall.
al - le - lu - ia, ba - by in the swad - dling clothes!
rall.
cresc. al fine
Ped.

THE WINDS OF BETHLEHEM

Text: Winifred M Letts
Music: Charles Villiers Stanford (1852-1924) arr. Neil Jenkins

dim.
ten.
four great winds came hand in hand and stood a-bout the ho - ly child.
p
Man.
f
p
The four great winds, their pi - nions furled, came soft-ly in with hum - ble
Ped.
Man.
f
tread; they saw the ma-ker of the world u-pon his low-ly man-ger bed.
Ped.
Man.
p
The south wind looked with ra-diant eyes u-pon this king so small and

sweet; he soft - ly sang him lul - la - bies, and knelt a - dor - ing at his
Ped.
feet. The west wind like a shep - herd clad had brought his
Man.
pas - toral pipes to play; he piped his mu - sic wild and glad un -
til the sha - dows fled a - way. The north wind
f
f
Ped.

bowed and knelt him down to gaze u - pon the sight so fair; he
gave the babe the fros - ty crown that lay u-pon his tan - gled
hair.
Man.
p
Be-fore that shrine the east wind bent, he had strange
p
Ped.
gifts be-yond all price, of gold and gems of
cresc.
cresc.

f
O - ri-ent, and gems and frank-in-cense and spice.
f
Man.
p
There was no wind on
dim.
p
Più lento
f
sea or land, but round a-bout the man - ger bed; the four great
f
Ped.
ff
winds stood hand in hand and wor - shipped there with wings out - spread.
ff

THE FIRST MERCY

Text: Bruce Blunt (1899-1957)
Music: Peter Warlock (1894-1930) arr. Charles Macdonald

child was born in our house, and the bright eyes of us three peeped at his na -
ti - vi-ty.
pp
Hands of peace u - pon that place
Gt.
Sw.
Sw.
pp
Man.
hushed our be - ings for a space – qui - et feet and fol - ded wing, nor a sound of
p sempre legato
a - ny-thing.
With a mov - ing star we crept
p
Ped.

clo - ser when the ba - by slept; men who guar - ded where he lay moved to frigh - ten
us a - way.
Gt.
Sw.
mf
But the babe, a - wa - kened, laid
Ped. 16´
mp
love on things that were a - fraid: with so sweet a ges - ture he called us to his
Man.
Ped.
com - pa - ny.
mf
f
p
mp
–16´
+16´

THE SONG OF SIMEON

Text: Peter Cornelius (1824-1874) trans. Neil Jenkins
Music: Peter Cornelius (1824-1874) arr. Neil Jenkins

Christ - child, new-born in Beth - le - hem. And at the tem - ple
p
Ped.
por - tal the a - ged Si - me - on took up this lit - tle
Man.
Ped.
mor - tal, sweet Ma - ry's first - born son. U - pon that face a -
Man.
sce - tic a re - ve - la - tion broke; and, struck with zeal pro -
cresc.
cresc.

poco rit.
a tempo
p
phe - tic, these rev'rent words he spoke. 'Now let-test thou thy
poco rit.
a tempo
p
Ped.
ser - vant, hi - ther de-part in peace. For I have seen sal -
cresc. poco a poco
va - tion be - gin and ne - ver cease: thy peo-ple Is - rael's
cresc. poco a poco
Man.
f
glo - ry, which hence-forth shall be heard in ho - ly gos - pel
f

sto - ry, ac-cor-ding to thy word.'
f
dim.
mp
With won-der past all
p
tel - ling they pon - dered on that word; then to their hum - ble
poco rit.
dwel - ling they took the lit - tle Lord.
poco rit.
pp

FLING OUT YOUR WINDOWS WIDE

Text: Arthur Thomas Quiller-Couch (1863-1944)
Music: Charles Villiers Stanford (1852-1924)

rall.
a tempo
f
D.C.
p
sa - tis - fied, in ex - cel - sis glo - ri - a!
un - dis - mayed, in ex - cel - sis glo - ri - a!
3. 'How shall we
Ped.
f
mf
find his man - ger - bed?' There shines a star a - bove his head; and
mf
p
Man.
choirs of view - less Che - ru - bim shall guide you to that hum - ble
p
inn: then sing, and rest you com - for - ted, in ex - cel - sis glo - ri -

a!
'And is it he that should be sent?' Three kings came
pp
Ped.
Man.
cresc.
from the O - ri - ent, a - rid - ing with the to - kens three, from
cresc.
Ind, Ca - thay, and A - ra - bye: then sing, and rest you con - fi - dent,
in ex - cel - sis glo - ri - a!
f
'What bring - eth he, the
f
Ped.
Man.

p
new - born King?' Lo! all good gifts there are to bring; 'tis
p
poco rall.
he shall turn your tears to mirth, and send good - will and peace on
poco rall.
Più lento
earth: then kneel, and rest you, wor - ship-ping, in ex - cel - sis glo - ri -
Tempo I
a!
p
pp
Ped.

O HOLY NIGHT

Text: J S Dwight (1813-1893) adapted Neil Jenkins
Music: Adolphe Adam (1803-1856) arr. Neil Jenkins

world in sin and er - ror pin - ing till the Re-
light of the star a-bove them gleam - ing had led the
v.2
deem - er should come u-pon the earth.
wise men from the O - rient land.
v.2
pp
The
The
wea - ry world with trem - bling hope re-joi - ces, for
King of kings lay in a low - ly man - ger, to
pp
yon - der breaks a new and glo - rious morn!
save our sin - ful souls and be our friend.

Solo
Chorus S A
mf
pp
mf
Fall on your knees! O hear the an - gel voi - ces! No - el! No - el! O night, when Christ was born! No - el! No -
He knows our need, he guards us all from dan - ger; No - el! No - el! Be - fore him let us bend! No - el! No -
Fall on your knees! O hear the an - gel voi - ces! No - el! No - el! O night, when Christ was born! No - el! No - el! No -
He knows our need, he guards us all from dan - ger; No - el! No - el! Be - fore him let us bend! No - el! No -

* If sung as a solo, take top line of Chorus part.

cresc.
night, when Christ was born! No - el! No-
fore him let us bend! No - el! No-
cresc.
night, when Christ was born! No - el! No -
fore him let us bend! No - el! No -
cresc.
v.2
dim.
rit.
a tempo
el! O night when Christ was born.
el! Be - fore him let us bend!
v.2
dim.
div.
el! O night when Christ was born.
el! Be - fore him let us bend!
rit.
a tempo
dim.
ff marcato
tr
1.
D.S.
2.